Sun and Earth

(F)

Contents

T3-BWQ-495

The Sun 2

Sunrise, Sunset 4

Across the Sky 6

What Really Moves? 10

Glossary 16

Jason Powe

The Sun

The sun gives heat and light to Earth.
There would be no life on Earth
without the sun.

The sun is in the sky every day.
Even on stormy days, the sun
is shining above the clouds.
It is still giving heat and light
to Earth.

Sunrise, Sunset

Day begins when the sun rises.
It ends when the sun sets.
The sun rises early in the morning.

In the evening, the sun sets.
After sunset, the sky will get dark.
This is the start of night.

Across the Sky

In the morning, the sun is near the **horizon**. The horizon is the line where land and sky seem to meet.

Then the sun seems to travel across the sky.
The sun seems to follow the same path each day.

Sky

Horizon

Earth

All morning, the sun seems
to climb higher in the sky.
By noon, it is at its highest point.

In the afternoon, the sun seems
to move lower in the sky.
By evening, the sun is near
the horizon again.

What Really Moves?

The sun does not move
across the sky.
It is Earth
that moves.
Earth is moving
all the time.

Every minute of every day,
Earth **rotates**.
To rotate is to spin like a top.
Earth takes 24 hours to spin
all the way around one time.

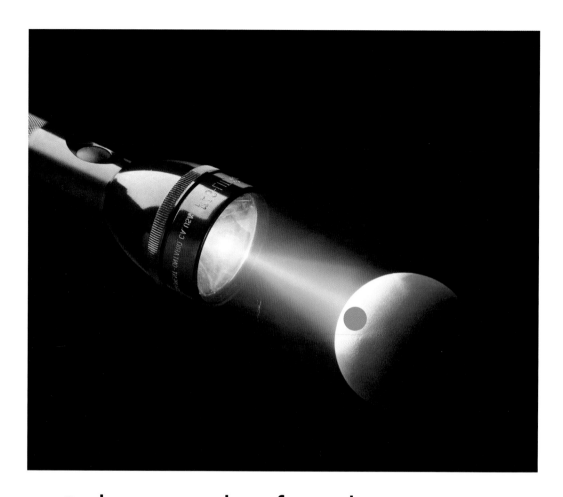

Only one side of Earth at a time faces the sun.
It is day on that side of Earth.

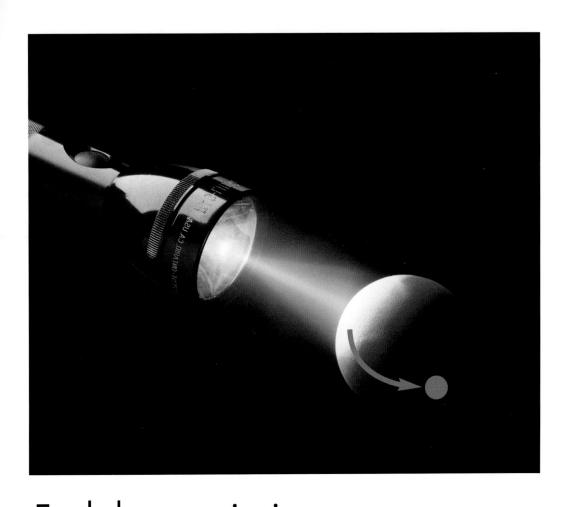

Earth keeps spinning.
That side of Earth turns away
from the sun.
Now it is night on that side of Earth.

Is it day or night right now?
It is both!
At any time, part of Earth faces
the sun.
It is day there.

At that same time, another part
of Earth faces away from the sun.
It is night there.
This is how day and night happen
at the same time.

Glossary

horizon the line where land and sky seem to meet. It is not a real line.

rotate turn around a center, like a top

sunrise the time of the day when the sun first appears on the horizon

sunset the time of day when the sun seems to reach the horizon and then disappears